# My Dandelion Darlings

A work of poetry

**By Morgan McCoy**

Published by Morgan McCoy 2020 Lulu Press

ISBN 978-0-359-12229-5

# Table of contents

Illustrations by: Jordyn Love.

I dedicate these poems to whom I love, loved and will love. Daddy, Grandma Lois and Uncle Jeff... Thank you for always chasing my frown away.

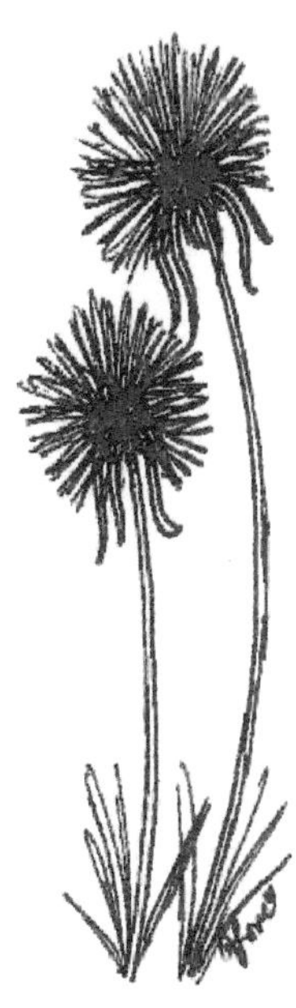

**<u>And so I gave you my heart…what else could I do with it?</u>**

# Introduction

It's funny how life works.

I've written poetry well before I could fully articulate my feelings. I have and most likely will always be a hyper emotional human being. What I've just begun to reconcile myself with is being ok with feeling whatever I'm feeling. I think that's why God gave this to me, poetry. He knew my crazy self would need an outlet for all the hate I'd feel. For all the love and lost I'd encounter. He knew I'd need these dandelion lines to figure out my shame, sadness and my joy. It is so like Him to disguise himself in between the lines and give me light. That's what these poems are: just a little light.

When you read these words you may find someone you know. I hope you find who you're looking for. I pray you find yourself. If only for just a moment, I hope they give you enough light to make a wish.

## Darling 1

If life were different.
If this time
Was not of our own doing,
I could easily
Say far more than
3 words
To you.

**All of The Days**

There are days
When your memory feels safe.
I hide
In the sound of your laugh
Let it fall softly on me,
Let it wash away all the hurt of yesterday.
There are days
When the memory of you feels good,
Like fire on cold bones
And I remember late nights or early mornings
Long buried.
And I could almost touch you.
And I could almost hear you.
And I could almost believe
You were here.
We are here,
And everything makes sense.
You never were good at goodbyes.
There are days
When your memory tears
And bares me.
Leaves me wanting
And I'm shivering.
There are days when that laugh haunts me
Like echoes off hollowed caverns
And I can't take it.
Break my eardrums just to make it.

And I'd rather forget the phone calls
Burn the notes and all the pictures,
And I can't touch you,
And I can't hear you,
And I can't believe,
You're not here.
We aren't here.
And nothing makes sense,
I was never good at saying goodbye.
There are days
Gathered together like dandelions
That I wish for you.
Some days I am angry
And sad,
Some days I don't fight the glad
And I laugh.

**Ornaments**

She said she has a hole in her heart
And she can't fix it.
Let the gift of her time and her spine
Be torn like cheap wrapping paper
Torn, tattered under toddler minded fingertips.
And she's got paper cuts of her own.
She's worked herself down to the rib,
3 pieces of tape won't hold her soul together
But she's too stubborn
Too proud
Too Ebenezer
And she's convinced herself that her present
Dictates her Eve.
So she keeps eating that same sugar plum of unbelief.
She's afraid of being returned
Before morning
So why even place herself under His tree.

He said
He's got a hole in his heart
And he can't fix it.
He's been too silent in his not so Holy night,
Lost his carol,
Resolved himself to back pews
And coal filled shoes
So all he leaves is black soot
And unlit flames.

He's ashamed,
Broken gingerbread of a man
And he can't seem to un-grinch himself
Won't un-lynch himself
So he stands just close enough to the altar to see
But he won't place himself under the tree.

We have a hole in our heart
And we can't fix it.

We can't fix what we broke
With our own hands,
No man can.
That's why he wrapped himself in flesh!
Morning star
Broke night in a manger.
He gave us such a perfect gift.
All that mercy,
All that grace,
He loves so vastly
That his plan from the beginning
Swaddled
The lamb
The great I am
Was always to fill up my empty space.
He knew, cooing amongst the ox and mule
That one day,
He'd raise himself up on a tree
On Calvary's hill

Red tinsel and all
So when I fall
I wouldn't have to stay there.
He bared all my wrong
So I could belong.
He made a way!
And if he is the most grandest of Christmas trees
Let me be His ornament,

You've got a hole in your heart
But it doesn't have to bleed
You think you're too broken
Too marred to give to him
But what love
He loves
And he choose you
Let him lace you to his salvation
Just embrace it,

I had a hole in my heart
And I couldn't fix it
So I let him change me
Rename me
Place me perfectly

Now I'm hooked,

## Darling 2

I felt the earthquake of your hello
And now my goodbye
Is always in search
Of your fault lines

## Darling 3

The clasp of your
Fingers
The lace of your hand
That's what I think of in between
Hello,

## Flecks of Gold

I'm not sure
But maybe
Maybe you're made of God.
Maybe I'm bias
Because I love you
And my daddy lent me the silhouette
Of your face.
Maybe it's
All that forgiveness in your eyelashes,
You don't mask your care.
Maybe,
Maybe it's
All that wisdom in your pupils.
You see us
You dilate my heart
And I'm never afraid of how open you
Leave me.
Don't leave me.
I hope you believe me.
Maybe it's the way your silence booms like My
savior's whisper,
Or how you remind me of canaries singing.
You tend to drown out all that ringing
Of this jilted
Tilted place we call now.
Maybe you're made of morning
Yeah,

That's it.
I see the sun in you.
Maybe you have angels for sons
And stars for daughters.
Maybe you're married to the moon,
All these maybes.
All these maybes
And all that I lack
Don't sway me from the fact
That I hope
There is more Mable in me than
There is marrow.
Maybe more than just the gap in my teeth,
Because I'm pretty sure
You're golden.
And maybe
Maybe that makes the rest of us worth Something.
And I'm ok with being a piece of you
I think it's the best part.

## **Good morning**

I know it's been a while,

I know it's been a while since
You felt good morning.
Been a while since
You forgave yourself.
All that breaking left you
Holey,
You've been listening to those cracks again.
Let them tell you what you're lacking in,
How faulty you are,

You can't be used by Him?
So
You let them use you,
Abuse you!
All that shattering.
You took hammer to your soul
Years ago,
And you think your eardrums are ruptured.

Like your heart.
You can't hear him,
Can't feel him
You're so broken
Now those whispers scream.
You forgot that you don't belong to them!

Forgot those nails,
Forgot those nails,
Pressed against wood and flesh.
How he hung
Like the sun
With every right to break your night.
You forgot that falling
Doesn't make you fallen
Unless you lie down
And this is not where we rest.

I know it's been a while love
But let me remind you,
His cross doesn't leave splinters
It makes whole.
I know it's been a while love
But let me remind you
How his blood crowned us
And bound us,
I know it's been a while love
But let me remind you,
He rolled the stone away
Buried all our sin in a tomb
He has no intention on visiting

No matter how rent
And rived,
I am alive

And if I could just make it there.
Place my face there,
At a altars arc
What will yesterday be?
All that mercy for you and me,

I know it's been a while,
But we can start today.
Lay all our pieces, chipped hearts and fractured vessels
In the carpenter's hands.
Say good morning

## Darling 4

You washed away all those scars called years
And dirt.
Washed them clean,
Like your love was rain.
Thank you for the storm
In you.

**Why you love me**

I'm not sure how you love me,
But you love me.
You love me
Like wind,
Blowing kisses over rolling hills
Causing all my chills to make home of you.
You love me like tulip bulbs
Before morning
Before dawn breaks their petals
And calloused hands pick them for I'm sorry bouquets.
You love me like the sun
Blaring, bold,
Bonding light to my dark places like cement.
You love me
And that should be enough
Especially because I'm marred
And scarred
And scared
Because you love me bare
And no one sees me like you.
My ocean heart pulls at your current
And I could drown
But you are my rescue
I'm not sure
I'll probably never understand,
But you love me
You love me like,

## Round and Round We Go

If you'd obliged,
I'd give you the sweetness of my words
And pray my pen not to be a liar.
I want to write you words that sound like hymns and taste like peaches,
Give you lines that growl like lions and moonlight as jaguars on Sundays.
They will stroll down river walks and downtown streets for you,
They will bleed blue and riot red like Detroit marches.
These words will capitalize themselves for no reason other than the want,
For you to read,
And if you refuse to open your eyes
My darling
They will write themselves into
Braille on the palm of my hand to give me cause to beg for your fingertips.
They will pick up oars and paddle boats across the ocean of you,
Just to pattern their cadence from your waves. I will write for you until the daffodil in your eyes turn golden at the placement of each comma,
And you are angered by my use of periods.
Each constant is yours,
I know you won't ask
But
I will gladly give you my vowels.
I adore you.

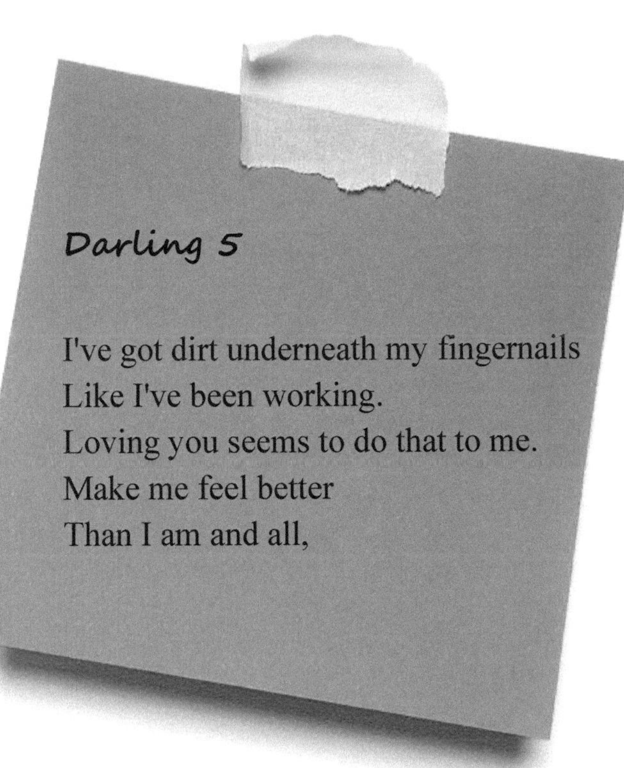
Darling 5
I've got dirt underneath my fingernails
Like I've been working.
Loving you seems to do that to me.
Make me feel better
Than I am and all,

## You Remind Me

Hey momma,
I am in awe of you.
I think I'll pride you in the tone of my skin,
Celebrate you like confetti freckles
And birthday marks.
All that marring making me
The only kind of beautiful
I ever want to be.
They say
I look like my daddy
And that's cool and all,

But
My momma,

My mother is like a nail,
Piercing
Petite
And holding us together.
I've hung pictures of what I should be
On her head.
I have given her many a migraine
With no Tylenol inkling of I'm sorry.
Yet she doesn't mind showing me mercy
Every time my canvas doesn't resemble
My reflection.
Every time I pressure her anchor,
Weigh her heavy
She roots me
And calls me Mona Lisa.
My mother looks like grace,

My momma
Tends to leave me
Misty,
When I think
I am not good enough
Not strong enough
Not clean enough
And I've done enough
To give up
I am reminded
By the forgiveness in your eyes.
They tell stories of falling
And standing
And I don't feel alone
And I don't feel defeated.
Now these tears
Baptize
Because my momma
Fought these same lies.
Still,
She knows how to mean I love you!
And when she smiles
I feel worth something,
Like there's hope for me.
My momma looks like compassion,

My mom taught me what truth looks like.
I watched the soles of her feet
Meet the indention of my savior's
Time
And time again.
Heard the truth in her prayers,
Felt the truth her altars bared.

Tasted truth in her chicken spaghetti,
She's done more than fill my belly
She gave me family!
My mother looks like peace,

It has taken me far too many Sundays,
Too many bad days
And good days unembraced.
Too many intentional words
Too many conversations missed
Too much silence.
I want you to know
You are the Melody in my symphony
The rise and fall.
I hope I sing you well enough
For others to understand
Yes, I know
I get my eyebrows from my daddy
But momma you have always been the light in my eyes
And I hope one morning
When I wake
I will look more like you
Than I did yesterday,
Because momma
You look like God to me.

**Granny's Smile**

I’ve never seen my grandma without a smile.
She wears it often
And brilliantly.
She wears it like her smile isn’t just for her,
Grandma you smile like you're the
Only umbrella
In the middle of a storm
That smile keeps dry.
She keeps me warm
That smile saves me.

But sometimes
Sometimes
I wish I had the capacity to be her rain jacket.
I want to cover you.
Let her button me
For just a moment,
I want to let her lean
Because I know behind that
Elephant ivory smile,
So much like my mother's
Like my Auntie’s,
That smile I'm still trying to master
Is a woman so strong she’s weary.
And I know I can’t carry you
But I’d like to show her
Though genetics didn’t favor me enough
To lend me your grin
I think we share the same back.

Grandmother,

Let me be your chair on open carports
Take rest in me.
I'd like to be your cold glass of tea.
Yes granny,
Grandmothers
Especially southern ladies like yourself
Should drink sweet tea
And laugh
They should laugh
And talk sweet and slow
Like the extra sugar at the bottom of your glass

But you,
You are no typical grandmother are you?
You work hard like the sun rising
You don't know any other way to be.

One day
I will tell my children
That you never had the heart to take switch to my hind.
And me and Dee never saw that cockroach,
But you'd threaten me with the disappearance of that smile.
I will tell them
How you left pockets in your stories,
Like grandfather's island
And cookies on your counter for little miss piggy.
And when they make me angry
I will try my hardest to be like you;
Honest and
Stern
But never deafening.
I will tell them their grandmother is my peridot,

My August morning.
And when I tuck them in
Or wave goodbye,
Or say hello,
Or dry their tears
I will try to mimic your umbrella smile.

Grandma I've never seen you without a smile
The day the tilt in your lips starts to fade
I will sit on an open porch and cover my eyes.

**Home**

When you speak,
When you laugh,
When your eyes open in the morning
My rib cage smiles,
Opens itself up and welcomes you
Like it knew you were home and it made
Room for your arrival.

You my darling are
The sun rising after too much darkness.
You are day break,
You are spring in a lifetime of winters
And I
Well I am thankful for this season.

And I don't know how you thank a flower for blooming
Or the stars for their light,
I don't know how
I can thank you for your beauty,
Or for all the God in you
Other than to say
For the rest of my life
I will love you like the sky is falling and you are shelter.

There is no place like home!

And no matter what this life brings
When you speak
When you laugh
When your eyes open in the morning
My rib cage will smile
And open itself up.
It will welcome you.
We will always be home
Together.

## You Can Have All The Hellos

Hello,

The syllables hiding under my damaged
Heart
Attack the roof of my mouth
Like Hiroshima bombs
Waiting to lay waste to the notion
That they belong to any other flesh and bone
Other than you.
And I live in a constant state
Of Floridian fear
And merriment that lands me.
And all of a sudden I realize I've been flying
Ever since that word tumbled out of my marrow in your direction.
My ribs ache when I speak to you,

Hola
I am trapped quite contently underneath the umbrella of your laugh,
Breaking through the storm of me
While simultaneously drenching me.
Can we dance in the rain?
I can't dance
Not really
But you salsa my syntax smoothly into this story I didn't dream of.
Oh how I dream you!
Wide awake

I dream you ,
And now all my poems are jealous of your name.
My ribs ache when I think of you,

Bonjour
Guten Tag
Nǐ hǎo
Salām!
Kon'nichiwa
I am not quite ready
To stop saying hello to you
To us
And whatever this will be.

I have glanced,
I can't linger because you drown me.
Yes,
I have glanced into the hickory of your eyes
And found shelter in how they see me.
You see me,
Broken boned and building.
And I have a problem,
A candescently beautiful problem.
I have these ruinated ribs
And they only want to live hello in you,
Are they welcomed?

## Darling 6

Drown it.
Hold it deep and long.
Take its breath away,
Then breathe my
Love.
Breathe, don't sigh
Some things just have to die,

Darling 7

Can i be dust again?
Marrow.
All this flesh gets in
The way
Of our love story,

**Sometimes**

Sometimes
Only sometimes,
When I'm afraid that when my lips part
Tears will fall instead of nouns.
Or fist will lay instead of punctuation marks.
Sometimes
When the hurt overwhelms me,
Numbs me
Or joy stills me
Stuns the movement from my jaw.
Sometimes,
When these feet get heavy
And they can't carry
And my knees are light
And without bend
And I try to mend my own heart,

Silly girl don't you remember?

You never learned how to sew

Just sometimes
Not nearly enough
But sometimes I look up
I look up
And i can care less how much ache the arch of my neck creates
It does not matter!
My eyes
They see the glory
Hidden behind the clouds

Somewhere out there
Over my promise.
I look up
And in my choice to stay quiet
I find that I have also chosen
Something far more precious
I have chosen you,
In the stillness of my hurt
In the quiet of my pain
In the hello of my thanking joy
Please
Please don't let the choice of you
Ever become
Sometimes.

## Darling 8

It anchors me,
The knowing you'd find me.
More so
That I could never be lost
From
You,
Yet you hold me like we
Are saying hello after passed
Time.

## Darling 9

Of all the hands
In all the world
I am glad it was yours
to hold mine.
If only for a moment
This little while smiles like eternity

**On The 20**

I met a boy today.
He made flowers out of foil
And he said Hi to me 6 times
In 10 minutes
I counted.
His smile
Was unfiltered
You could see the sunshine through where he was missing.
I don't know his name
And he doesn't know mine.
We didn't make introductions like you would normally.
No,
He just sat down
Said hi
And laid his head on my shoulder,
And I doubt his head was as heavy as mine is
Not enough time to accumulate years of weight,
Doubt,
Worry,
Shame,
No his head couldn't have been as heavy as my heart is.
But all the same he made rest on me.
And I wanted to open my arms to him
Hold him just a little bit closer.
Tell Him the world is as ugly as you can imagine.
Yes there are monsters
And tragedies!
No they will not treat you fairly.

They will not understand you.
They will hate you.
And call it freedom of whatever.
But there are bright spots,
Like little boys with big smiles and friendly hellos.
Yes little one there are moments of Eden
In this unattended garden.
I wanted to love Him openly,
But because that would have been socially unacceptable
I offered him a smile.
And I'm sure it wasn't as illuminating as His
But I offered it to him with every ounce of gratitude I had.
And I wanted to say thank you.
Thank you for all your care not.
All your joy.
Thank you for laying your head on my shoulder and giving me rest,
Thank you little boy with the sun trapped in his smile

You said hi to me in God's voice
6 times,
In ten minutes.

I counted

## Darling 10

When did it get complicated?
I suppose it was the day
I said don't leave me
And you knew,
You knew you were already gone.

**If I Fall**

I've spent most of my days running
Or hiding.
I have spent
And spun
Hours
With my head pounding
Against the pavement,
Against my chest.
I fight headaches that think themselves
Heart aches,
Or maybe heart aches
Confused for migraines.
All I know is that my soul
Use to hurt.
And my mom never bought Band-Aids.
And I've almost overdosed on pain pills,
Trying to kill
All this deadness inside of me
Trying so desperately
I tripped over so many others
My ankles are broken
Like my heart.
But for you I'm willing to fly

I'm sorry.
I say that too often,
I'm so sorry,
For being sorry
I'm trying my hardest not to be her
And she scares me
Living behind my scarred earlobes

And fragile smile
Every time I gain a mile
She reminds me
How much I hate running
And there's no bases to turn
But I've caught glimpses of home
And I all I know is
I want to be there.
I want you,
So this is my last sorry
For you I'm willing to fly
I don't need a parachute

I've grown cautious
I'm a worn page
All scattered
Tattered
Dog eared
And used for kindle
But if your furnace is where my ashes rest
Then
Then let me fall with the cinder
I've always wanted to fly
But if I fall
If I fall
Let it be at your feet
If I fall
When I fall
I know you'll catch me
I'm letting go
Don't let me blow in the wind

## Darling 11

There is a lot of i and you here
But there is no we.
There I've said it,
I want you here,
There I've said it.
Did you here me?

## Parachutes

My dad packed my parachute
Told me to wear it
Like my life depended on it
Because one day I'd jump.

There are some things that
Don't need to be said
Like,
The sound of boots
After 6'oclock.
It was the sweetest hello I've ever heard
And he didn't need to speak.

He packed my chute
When he laughed,
Taught me to enjoy the clouds
On the way down.
He packed my chute
When I caught quick peeks
Underneath my sheets
Of him and momma dancing,
Al Green or something slow like that.
He didn't say
Anything,
But he spun her
Held her like he was saying
One day,
He should hold you like this.
Make you laugh like this.
Turn your world like this.

My dad packed my parachute
My dad
Packed my parachute and told me to wear it
Like my life depended on it
Because one day
I'd jump.

But there are some things that need to be said,
Some things
Need to be tattooed on little girl's eardrums.
Played like snares and
High hats.
Reverberating to little girl souls
So when little girls turn into women
They don't have little girl holes
In their parachutes.
All those holes make it hard for safe landings.
Some things must be heard
And breathed in
If you want her to understand
The things not spoken.
Tell her!
Tell her she is spectacular
Before anyone can break
The rose in her glasses.
Tell her you see her
So when others do
They won't become mirrors,
She'll already know what adoration
Feels like and won't mistake it
For polyester.
Tell her she can do anything
But everything isn't for
Her.
And then,
Tell her the difference.
Tell her to tie her shoes
So she won't trip on her journey
And when she does
Because she will,
She will remember how to pull the ties of herself together.
Loop the bunny ears around her tragedy
And make bows out of her mistakes.

Dads should pack their little girl's parachutes

Let her dance on your shoelaces
Pack her parachute.
Tell her she's beautiful in the morning,
Pack her parachute.
Show her what conversations with God sound like,
Pack her parachute.
Tell her no
And why.
Hold her hand
And let her run.
You should pack her parachute.
Tell her to wear it
Like her life depended on it
Because one day she'll jump
And it will probably be
Without you.

My dad packed my parachute,
Though he didn't get to have
All these conversations.
I didn't get to hear or see
All his hope,
I felt it
The day I pulled the string
And the wind took me.
Because that's what dads do,
They pack your parachute.
They turn falling
Into flying.

**Ray**

I find myself
Constantly
With much thought
Reaching
Trying to tug you down
Trying to spread you across my cheeks,
I've never wanted freckles so desperately
I just want to be reminded,
You're a part of me.
But
I can't see you.
Not yet,
Not for, too long now.
I've been inside
My own head
Buried underneath my blanket of
Too close to sin.
And if you were any other
You would have left me
By now
Blessed for me,
My life,
You are the only exception.
I know you hear me.
I'm on my way.

I hate the night
I hate that you feel gone
You surround me
But you feel so far.
Hey love
Don't leave.

How many times have I said that?
Hey love don't
Leave me.
Help me not to walk away,
Bolt my heart to you.

Because I get so afraid of great
But that's not who you are
You'll never be.
You don't beg
You wait patiently
And I'm not use to gentlemen
Who listen.
I just need my life to catch up to my lips.
And if you were any other
You would have left me
By now
Blessed for me,
My All,
You're not man made.
I'm sorry I'm late.

My whole life
All I've ever wanted
Was a little sun
Thought I'd be content with just
A little ray.
But you don't come in pieces.
And I'm all in pieces.
But I'm getting there
To you
To us.

I just want to sit in the sun.

**Where We Snap**

This is where we snap.

My folded edges
All bent and
Pressed orange
Are smudged and almost misshapen.
So close to red
I might be bleeding.
I won't mistake this for the sunrise
I don't do so well with waiting
But these pieces don’t work
They don’t labor and plow
No those pieces don’t grow anything
Don’t build anything
Not with my pieces.

Together
We make a jumbled mess of a picture
My peace
Doesn’t home here.
No
This is not my photograph.
This is where we snap

You can’t just belong to anything
Just anywhere.
But sometimes
I am overwhelmed with the need
To fit,
Not in
But within.

I want to
I want to be melded into your color scheme
Want to fade and breathe
And come alive in the picture
That is without doubt us.
We,

I want to snap,
Snap into the curves of your purpose.
In your hollowed out
Rounded edges
Is where I fit,
Where we fit.
Makes things complete,
And I can see
Yeah
I can see the picture now.

Yeah,
This picture makes sense
I always wondered were that blue was leading
This is where we snap.

## Darling 12

One day,
With no shades at all
You will blind me
The world will slip away
And I'll be radiant

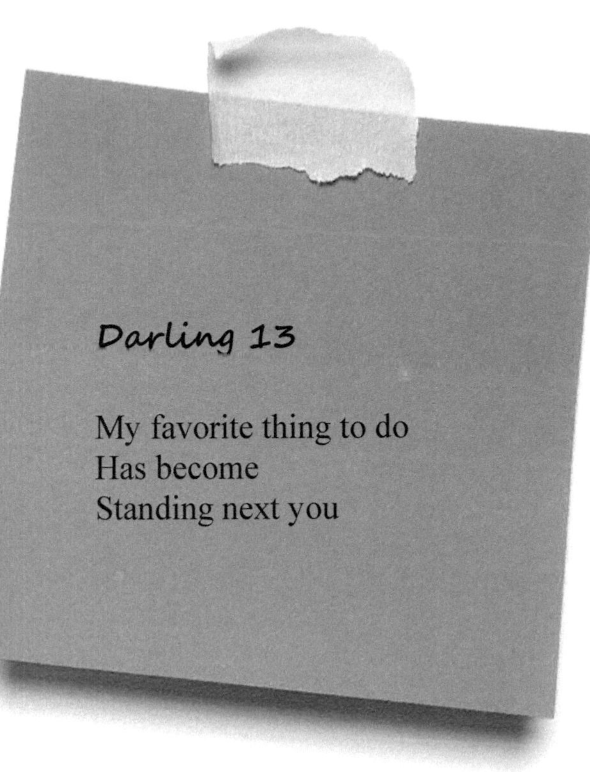
Darling 13

My favorite thing to do
Has become
Standing next you

**Untitled**

You make me taller.
And that is no small feat
Stretch me,
And I am goliath.
I am never wounded by you
But you heal me
Completely.
Turn this weary into wonder
I have never wanted to choose someone
Constantly,
Without thought
Without falter.
I am
Dust to your diamond
You make me smile
And cry
And try
Oh, how you make me want to try
To better
Apple holding Eve I am
But you have always been more than able
You are my sun
No
You are my dandelion
Darling.
Turning wishes into prayers
Prayers into answers
Answers into home.
I am home in the field of you
I won't question that.
I'll just rest here for a while
After forever.

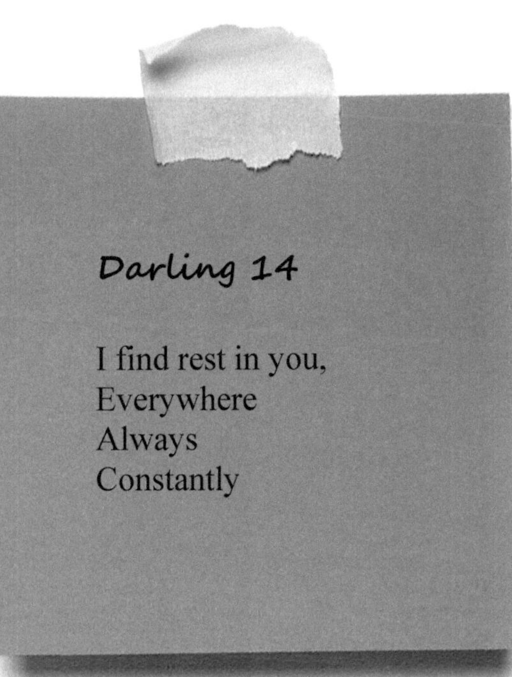
Darling 14

I find rest in you,
Everywhere
Always
Constantly

www.ingramcontent.com/pod-product-compliance
Ingram Content Group UK Ltd.
Pitfield, Milton Keynes, MK11 3LW, UK
UKHW041838200726
13854UKWH00003BA/1200